Table of Contents

For over 30 years, Dr. Will Horton has been the leader in the use of NLP and Hypnosis in the field of addictions, it is why he has lead an addiction seminar at our conference each year. Every year he adds new information, research, and science, such as what is in this book. Once again Dr. Horton breaks new ground with this ground breaking new work. If you or a loved one has an addiction do not read this book, devour it. Thanks again "Cowboy Doc" another great work! Elsom Eldridge Conference Director National Guild of Hypnotists.

"For 20 years, I've enjoyed discussing the topic of addictions with Dr. Will. He is knowledgeable both in the scientific theory as well as the practical realities of addiction. He is truly the go to guy in this arena"" Scott Sandland , CEO of HypnoThoughts

"For over a decade, Will Horton has been a resource and go-to expert on addictions for both myself, and members of our organization. Dr. Horton has the personal insight, expert training and real-world experience helping people leave addition behind them." Richard Nongard Founder International Certification Board of Clinical Hypnotherapists

This book is amazing in the breakthroughs it presents and the information about addictions in a new light. Direct, to the point and easy to read, if you are interested in addictions this book is for you. Dr. Horton's technique has saved many from addictions and now he adds a new layer to this once complex issue. He should be a requirement for anyone who wants to help people change! Adam Adams Master NLP & Hypnosis Trainer

From Dr. Will Horton:

I didn't get in trouble every time I drank, but every time I got in trouble, I was drinking.

It wasn't how much I drank; it's what the drink did to me.

It felt like I had a hole in my soul.

I had hollowness in my heart.

I felt empty on the inside years before I ever took that first drink. (or drug)

Those are statements made by people with an addiction, I said them repeatedly, and to all who has said something like this, this booklet was written. It is a small book, but its information is valuable beyond measure, if it is used to help someone recover from a seemingly hopeless state of mind, body, and spirit.

For over 35 years I have been in the addiction field, both as a client and as a healer. I have studied why some people seem to succeed easily at recovery and others struggle even though they do everything to the best of their ability.

With the recent breakthroughs in neuro-science we are beginning to understand what was once not understandable.

Read this book with an open mind, and if interested read "The Alcohol and Addiction Solution, Vol 2, Breakthroughs In Recovery".

This brings into the addiction world the breath taking science of neurology and its new areas. This is truly a brave new world and I welcome you to the new frontier.

All the best in your journey, it truly is a road less traveled.

May the sun be in your face, and the wind at your back.

Dr. Will Horton

Chapter one

1.0 Neuroscience addiction and recovery

We may think that the brain, once are damaged, may not repair itself. Breakthroughs in field of neuroscience have given it, that this is not true. Though, ones neurons may be damaged beyond state of recovery, the brain stems attempts to healing itself when damaged in making new connections with new neural pathways working-around. It is called neuroplasticity the moldabilty of the brain nerves.

1.2 What does neuroplasticity mean for addiction treatment?

When we develop a habit, the brain creates a path in itself in support of that habit. As we engage in the habit over and over again, the pathway becomes well-worn or stronger. This is similar to lifting a weight. If you lift a weight over and over, the muscle will get stronger. In many ways, addiction can be explained as a neuroplasticity event. The brain gets trained to do a particular behavior – use drugs or alcohol or gambling – eventually to the exclusion of all else. BUT, in treatment, we can retrain the brain, that is develop a new pathway that supports recovery. With intensive psychotherapy and other holistic interventions, we strengthen the new "recovery" loop within the brain. The brain then learns to enjoy recovery, those things that give us pleasure in our sober lives – family, work, interpersonal interactions. We retrain the brain and thus change our lives.

1.3 How does the brain's function have a role in relapse?

Essentially, in addition, the pleasure centers of the brain are hijacked by the addiction. Eventually, it is only the addictive behavior that brings the addict any sense of joy, or at least freedom from pain. This is not only a biochemical process; drugs themselves affect the brain's biochemistry, but also a process of habit. The addict's brain becomes accustomed to the addictive act being the source of pleasure – not family, friends, a good meal, or a job well done. We can retrain the brain and we can rebalance the addict's biochemistry, BUT, the old neuropathways, the old links between addiction and pleasure are still there. This is why we suggest complete abstinence from drugs and alcohol to addicts. It doesn't take much to jump start the old habit.

For example, you may not have been to your college campus in twenty years, but within minutes of arrival for a visit, it will become familiar to you – your old haunts, how to get around, etc. Addiction is no different. Recovery doesn't remove the addictive thought process; it just gives the addict an opportunity to change behaviors.

1.4 Behavioral sensitization

The learned behaviors seen in addiction involves a new technology of real-time functional magnetic resonance imaging biofeedback of brain activity Addicts have been shown to have poor ability to inhibit impulses, and this correlates with decreased frontal lobe activity. Normal subjects can activate frontal control mechanisms when attempting to inhibit sexual arousal, but cocaine-dependent patients are unable to inhibit craving when shown drug-related stimuli. By providing feedback of frontal activation, the patients will attempt to learn to activate inhibitory structures and inhibit drug craving. This represents a therapeutic attempt to introduce new learning to control addictive behavior. The continued study of the underlying mechanisms of plasticity will undoubtedly produce other novel pharmacological and behavioral treatments. Addiction is a disease of neuroplasticity. In the past, clinicians considered detoxification to be the treatment for addiction. However, detoxification is simply removal of the drug from the body and treatment of withdrawal symptoms. Now we know that the essence of addiction continues long after the last dose of the drug, often lasting for years.

A very interesting animal model of this approach has been illustrated by a series of experiments by Kailas el al. using rats trained to self-administer cocaine; they reported a reduction in glutamate in the brains of animals exposed to long-term cocaine and a disruption of glutamate homeostasis. Following withdrawal from chronic cocaine there is a marked imbalance in glutamate homeostasis, with both cysteine-glutamate exchange and glutamate uptake being reduced in the nucleus accumbency. Tolerance is manifested by reduced effects from a given dose that is given repeatedly, and "physical" dependence (not addiction) is manifested by withdrawal symptoms when the drug is stopped abruptly. This form of plasticity occurs in all individuals when certain drugs are taken repeatedly. Examples include prescribed medications such as β-blockers, antidepressants, sedatives, and opioids for pain, as well as commonly abused drugs such as alcohol, cocaine, and nicotine. The second form of neuroplasticity is manifested by compulsive drug-seeking behavior.

1.5 What then is interpersonal neurobiology as illustrated?

This was first demonstrated in animal models, and later shown in human addicts more than 35 years ago. Addiction is fundamentally a memory trace that manifests itself by reflex activation of brain circuits, especially the reward system, resulting in motivation to resume drug-taking behavior when drug related cues are encountered. Drugs that activate the reward system carry liability for the development of addiction, but vulnerability to this disorder is influenced by complex genetic and environmental variables.

A characteristic of all drugs that are abused by humans is that they activate dopamine circuits in brain reward systems by a variety of mechanisms. This has been demonstrated directly in animal models and indirectly in human brain imaging studies. Other neurotransmitters are also involved, but dopamine has received the greatest attention. While a given drug of abuse will tend to have very similar immediate effects in all users, only a minority of users progress to the stage of compulsive use or addiction. Two general forms of neuroplasticity can be demonstrated. The first, and most common, is tolerance accompanied by physical dependence.

Disruption of this process blocks the development of drug-associated plasticity such as behavioral sensitization. The latter is the increase in motor behavior in response to repeated, fixed doses of a stimulant.

Genes directly regulated by delta fops B appear to have different effects and may limit as well as promote drug reinforcement. The delta Fop B changes are temporary, with return to prior levels when the drug is no longer present. Thus, these transcription factor changes do not seem to underlie long-term neuroplasticity. Changes in neuronal morphology have also been noted in animals exposed to drugs that are abused. In the nucleus acumens, an increase in dendritic spine density has been reported in medium spiny neurons from rats self-administering cocaine. These changes persisted during abstinence, and may be involved in long-term changes associated with drug-seeking behavior. Changes in neuronal morphology have also been found in individuals chronically exposed to opioids.

Chronic morphine given to rats, for example, has been found to reduce dendritic spines (whereas stimulants increased spines) on ventral tegmental area neurons. Chronic morphine also reduces neurogenesis in the hippocampus. These changes may be the basis for the cognitive losses seen in some patients receiving chronic opioids for pain. Since the learned addictive behavior is thought to result from neuroplasticity such as that described above, it seems logical to consider reversal of these changes as a target for the treatment of addictive behaviors.

1.6 Addiction system activation

Evidence of the plasticity that has occurred with the development of addiction can be demonstrated by brain imaging studies that show rapid activation (increased blood flow to reward pathways) when drug-related cues are shown to addicts who have been free of drugs for at least a month. Even cues so brief that they do not reach consciousness can produce rapid activation. During brain reward system activation, the addict reports drug craving. The strength of the craving is related directly to the amount of endogenous dopamine released in reward structures, as measured by displacement of labeled raclopride in positron emission tomography studies

More direct studies of the plasticity induced by drugs of addiction can be seen in animal models. Shah am and colleagues have studied the relapse or reinstatement of drug-taking in rats trained to self-administer intravenous cocaine. Availability of cocaine is signaled by a light that the animal then associates with cocaine. After the behavior is well trained, the cocaine can be turned off; thus, pushing the lever no longer provides cocaine.

After the extinction process is complete, the animal can be tested for reinstatement by returning it to the drug-taking environment and giving the light cue. This is considered to be a model of "relapse" in human addicts. The intensity of relapse can be measured by the number of times the light causes the rat to press the bar despite not receiving any cocaine. Eventually, the unrewarded bar pressing stops. It was found that reinstatement occurred when rats were tested 1 week after extinguishing cocaine-seeking, but the reinstatement was significantly greater at 4 weeks, and progressively increased further if the rats were allowed to rest in their cages for up to 6 months before relapse testing. The strengthening of relapse tendency over time has been called "incubation" and is associated with increases in the levels of the growth factor brain-derived neurotropic factor in the ventral tegmental area and in the nucleus acumens, also found that exposure to cocaine cues increased extracellular signal-related kinase in central amygdala after 30 days of rest, but not after 1 day.

This shows that there is an active neuroplasticity process in the brain that increases over time and is manifested by increased cocaine-seeking behavior. Transcription factors have been observed to be changed by addictive drugs. A delta fop B accumulates in dopamine terminals in the cortex and striatum. All drugs of abuse tested produce an increase in delta Fogs B, which appears to be involved in the development of motivated behaviors.

The reward system, which developed early in evolution, reinforces adaptive behavior such as that leading to the acquisition of water, food, and sex. Drugs that directly activate the reward system may produce learning that diverts the individual to those behaviors that repeat the drug-induced feelings of reward. An important feature of this form of neuroplasticity is that it is stable and perhaps permanent. The dopamine release caused by a drug of abuse tends to be greater than that of natural rewards, and to continue with repeated exposure rather than diminish, as is the case with natural, expected rewards. Thus, the drug experience becomes associated with environmental cues and acquires increasing salience. Individuals who develop this neuroplasticity tend to suffer from a chronic illness with potential for relapse, even years after the last dose of the drug. Drug-taking then acquires more salience than natural or adaptive behaviors.

1.7 Synaptic nucleus

Taken together, the data above suggest the possibility that normalization of glutamate homeostasis in addicts might restore the ability to induce synaptic plasticity in the nucleus accumbency, which in turn could facilitate establishing behaviors that might compete with drug seeking. Exogenous N-acetyl cysteine is used for the treatment of hepatic failure in acetaminophen overdose. Thus, it was available to be administered to cocaine addicts presented with cocaine-related cues in an attempt to translate findings in the animal model to human addicts. Those treated with N-acetyl cysteine reported reduced desire for cocaine compared with the control group in another human study, N-acetyl cysteine was found to reduce pathological gambling and cigarette smoking further clinical trials are in progress

Chapter two

2.1 Brain functionality

Our brain and gut are intrinsically connected. We have 'gut feelings' about a person or event, and feel 'butterflies' in our stomach when something exciting happens. Neuroscientists have become increasingly aware that our gut may hold critical insights into brain function.

The gut itself has what has often likened to a mini-brain an extensive network of neurons called the enteric nervous system. The brain and enteric nervous system talk, and the shared communication line between the two are often called the gut-brain axis.

2.2 How can we change our gut micro biome?

I think of the micro biome like the different soils that plants grow in certain plants grow well in nutrient-rich compost, but they won't survive in dry, sandy soil. Western diets, especially those with low levels of fiber, have possibly reduced the diversity of micro biota over generations. By contrast, traditional foods high in fiber and low in sugar and fat increase micro biome diversity

2.3 So what can we do to ensure our micro biome supports our health?

Researchers suggest the diversity and function of micro biome are established by your genetic background and external factors, including the way you were delivered at birth and how you exercise. It's suggested the key determinant affecting the composition and activity of the gut micro biome is your diet explaining about 78.6% of variations in total gut micro biota.

We can influence the populations of gut microbes by making our gut environment hospitable to them by eating probiotic and prebiotic foods.

Probiotics are foods or dietary supplements containing specific gut-beneficial microbes (such as Lactobacillus or Bifid bacterium to stimulate the growth of these microorganisms in the gut. Probiotic-rich foods include live yogurt, kombucha, kamahi, and fermented vegetables such as sauerkraut.

Prebiotics are foods that stimulate the growth of beneficial bacteria. I think of them as the nutrient-rich fertilizer that helps plants grow. Prebiotic-rich foods include bananas, onions, wheat, flaxseeds, legumes, and leafy green vegetables, e.g., spinach, kale, and broccoli. Fermented foods contain microbes that aid gut health and are also prebiotic. The live bacteria have already worked.

2.4 The brain-gut-micro biome axis

There is another crucial player in the gut-brain conversation. Our intestines are home to an entire ecosystem of microbes that control digestion, fight pathogens, and modulate hormone and neurotransmitter production. The collective of these microbes is termed the 'gut micro biome'. An average person has about 1.5 kg of bacteria in their gut – similar to the weight of the brain! Gut bacteria also make the neurotransmitters including γ-amino butyric acid (GABA), serotonin, dopamine, and acetylcholine.Gut bacteria talk to the enteric nervous system and the brain, but the precise method of communication is unknown researchers call it 'black box connectivity.' Possible lines of communication include via hormones, immune signaling molecules, metabolic pathways, and via the vague nerve.

2.5 The gut-brain superhighway

The gut communicates with the brain via hormones released into the bloodstream that cross the blood-brain barrier, controlling our desire for food. For example, the gut hormone ghrelin tells us when we're hungry and other hormones such as glucagon-like peptide one influence satiety or tell us when we're full. Such hormones act on the reward-signaling neural circuits in the brain, explaining why food tastes better when we are hungry.

The gut also makes neurotransmitters, which are the molecules neurons use to communicate at synapses. One such neurotransmitter is serotonin. About 80% of the body's total serotonin is made in the gut; the rest is formed in the nervous system. In the stomach, specialized enterochromaffin cells lining the wall of the stomach produce and secrete serotonin where it plays the crucial role in controlling peristalsis the wave-like contractions of the gut walls that squeeze food along the digestive tract. Some neurons in the enteric nervous system also make and use serotonin as a neurotransmitter.

Note! The gut is not the brain's 'serotonin factory.' Neurons in the brain make their neurotransmitters. Also, gut-secreted serotonin and other neurotransmitters cannot cross the blood-brain barrier, so it's improbable gut serotonin directly influence brain function via the bloodstream.

2.6 How might gut bugs speak to the brain?

The gut provides an environment for bacteria to ferment digested food into all kinds of chemicals and molecules that inform the brain of our current nutritional state. As mentioned in the previous blog, the micro biome signals to the brain via pathways such as vague nerve, immune and hormone systems, and also via the production of bioactive microbial metabolites released into the bloodstream.

Short-chain fatty acids (SCFAs) are metabolites produced in the gut by microbial fermentation of undigested dietary fiber and complex carbohydrates. SFCAs can cross the blood-brain barrier and modulate brain activity to regulate appetite and food intake. In the brain, SCFAs are neuroprotective.

One such SCFA is butyric acid or butyrate. Butyrate is an anti-inflammatory agent in the brain and the gut and reduces levels of harmful toxins that can damage neurons. Butyrate also fortifies the blood-brain barrier by tightening connections between cells, which prevents harmful toxins from entering the brain causing neuron-damaging inflammation. A leaky blood-brain barrier is often seen in obesity and neurodegenerative disorders such as Alzheimer's disease. Butyrate also boosts the production of molecules that are important for neuroplasticity including brain-derived neurotropic factor (BDNF). Heightened levels of BDNF leads to enhanced memory performance in lab rats, Scientists have found that eating a junk food diets reduces SCFA levels, so it is essential to eat a healthy diet to maintain optimal brain function.

2.7 Squeaky clean mice

Much of the micro biome research to date has used germ-free mice raised in highly sterile conditions. Germ-free mice are born by Caesarean section, thereby preventing the transfer of microbes from their mother. They grow up inside sterile isolators, are fed purified food and water, and breathe filtered air. Germ-free mice offer a blank canvas when it comes to their gut micro biome.

Fecal micro biome transplants FMTs poo transplants into germ-free mice allow researchers to explore how a specific gut micro biome profile can change brain function. For example, after receiving a poo transplant, germ-free mice adopt the behavioral traits of the donor mouse. One study showed germ-free mice that received FMTs from stress-prone mice became more nervous in a new environment — essentially passing nervousness from their poo-donor. In comparison, germ-free mice receiving FMTs from more curious and interested mice became less anxious in strange situations.

These experiments suggest the presence and composition of gut micro biota provides a signal to the brain via the gut-brain axis that in turn modifies rodent emotions.

However, it's essential to understand that germ-free mice are not typical mice. Germ-free mice are reared in artificial 'bubble-like' environments in the absence of micro-organisms to shape their immune systems. Their behavior fundamentally differs from standard lab mice; particularly stress reactions and social responses.

2.8 May we balance the brain with bacteria?

Altering the micro biome through FMTs has potential to change brain chemistry. Case reports in humans suggest that FMTs may have therapeutic potential for disorders including autism, chronic fatigue syndrome and multiple sclerosis, but much more research is needed. There is a well-recognized 'gap' between rodent neuroscience research and application in humans.

In my next blog, I will discuss how scientists are manipulating the micro biome through the use of 'psychobiotics' to treat mood disorders and the use of probiotics and prebiotics as brain health supplements.

Our intestines are home to an ecosystem of trillions of microbes including bacteria, viruses, phages, fungi, protests, and nematodes. Dominant are bacteria from the families Formicates and Bacteriodetes. As I talked about in my last blog, the collective community of these microbes in the intestines is the gut 'micro biome.'

In this blog, we'll consider the gut micro biome from the perspective of obesity research. Changes in the gut micro biome are associated with several disease states including obesity. Obesity-associated microbes affect insulin resistance, inflammation, fat deposition, metabolism, and appetite. And the gut micro biome is becoming a target for new anti-obesity therapies.

2.9 How does the micro biome influence our health?

The gut micro biome responds to its surrounding environment including to the foods we eat. Healthy versus unhealthy diets have a profound effect on the micro biome including which species dominate.

For example, eating an unhealthy diet full of sugar and saturated fat alters the balance between 'good' Bactericides and 'bad' firm cutes bacterial species. Formicates are needed to digest fats, and eating a high-fat diet encourages their population to increase, leading in turn to weight gain. Bacteriodetes digest soluble fiber, so people who consume fiber-rich foods have more Bacteriodetes than formicates.

Research in germ-free mice, which lack gut microbes, found altering the balance between Bacteriodetes and formicates dictated how obese or lean mice became. And a propensity for obesity or leanness could be transmitted from mouse to mouse via gut microbes alone.

The brain regulates appetite, feeding behaviors, and energy balance, and although the gut micro biome contributes to obesity and metabolic syndromes such as diabetes, the exact mechanisms underlying this relationship are uncertain. To date, the link between the micro biome and obesity in humans is "weak."

Chapter Three

3.1 Newness and Challenge of diagnosis and treatment of mental illness

Psychology is uniquely positioned to maximize the revolution which is set to transform the diagnosis and treatment of mental illness and reverse the lack of significant progress made in curbing associated ill health and death over the past 100 years.

This specialty can influence "the development of a credible risk score coupled with some, or all of, cognitive training, psychosocial approaches, education, and the use of specially designed video and computer games" as well as promoting choices that can enhance neuroplasticity for, per Marian Diamond, "Enriching Heredity. Applying interventions in positive ways to enhance neuroplasticity, is the model proposed herein because it captures changes made in the Diamond lab. The only change in their enriched environment was having lab workers hold and talk with the rats; that "TLC" resulted in a fifty percent increase in longevity while maintaining plastic gains even in animals that lived to the equivalent of ninety human years, Diamond opined humans could enjoy these plastic gains at any age. She identified five essentials for a healthy brain: newness, challenge, exercise, diet, and love. Animal and human research has shown that environmental stimulation is critical for enhancing and maintaining cognitive function.

3.2 Cognitive function

Novelty, focused attention and challenge are essential components of enhancing cognitive function. The observed difficulty associated with the enjoyment of the task it functions as reinforcement for humans. Even when additional stimulation was not in provision until rats were middle-aged, an enriched environment resulted in a fivefold increase in neuronal phenotypes that was associated with significant improvements in learning parameters, exploratory behavior, and locomotors activity, In addition, these new and enriching experiences resulted in decreased age-dependent degeneration as shown by less accumulation of lipofuscin in the dentate gurus. These findings corroborate those of Diamond's work that ceroplastic gains with new and enriched environments are not limited to a brief "critical" period. The timing of enrichment has also been the focus of studies with humans.

Mayo Clinic Study of Aging is showing that academic and career achievements in the 75th percentile showed higher levels of cognition with a delay of cognitive impairment of 8.7 years as compared to individuals in the 25th percentile. This research involved 1,995 people without dementia aged 70–89, of whom only 277 had mild cognitive impairment (MCI). Since people whose intellectual enrichment focused in midlife also showed significant gains, newness, and challenge seen as a powerful way to lengthen the "healthy lifespan. In the Rush Memory and Aging Project, the 964 individuals without cognitive impairment had an average age of 78.7 years and an average of 14.6 years of education when they agreed to annual evaluation and brain autopsy at their death. At the beginning of the study they were asked if by the age of 18 they had foreign language instruction; if they had any music lessons; and if so, how many years of each. Throughout about six years of annual examinations, 396 individuals developed MCI.

The risk of MCI was about 30% less in those who before the age of 18 had had more than four years of foreign language training; the same finding was true of those who before 18 years of age had had more than four years of music lessons. When compared to people who had neither foreign language training nor music lessons before turning 18, the risk of MCI was about 60% less in individuals who had more than four years of both foreign language instruction and music lessons in their early years. It is unknown how much of this could have been mediated by the extent to which individuals used these skills during the intervening years between youth and being in the study. Music is a sophisticated and multisensory form of enrichment that has a positive influence on neuroplasticity in several regions of the brain because it requires integration of audiovisual information as well as an appreciation of abstract rules.

3.2 Magneto measures

Magneto encephalography measures with individuals with an average age of 26.45 found that the anterior prefrontal cortex played a central role and that the neuroplasticity response was more significant in musicians with long term training than was noted in those with short term training. After 4 months of piano lessons, people aged 60–84 years enjoyed improved mood, as well as significant improvements in the cognitive skills of attention, control, motor function, visual scanning, and executive functioning A recent review, found music training associated with enhanced cognition in a variety of musical and non-musical skills spanning from executive functions to creativity. Non-musician healthy individuals aged 60–84 responded to the background music of Mozart with a significant increase in their processing speed in comparison to the other three groups that had silence, white noise or the background music of Mahler. In the same study, both Mozart and Mahler as background music associated with better memory as compared to the groups tested with silence or white noise in the background. These scientists opined that the emotions induced by the music facilitated the memory advantage. Young, non-musician university students that listened to music while encoding had better word recognition than peers who kept in silence.

Enhanced activation of the dorsolateral prefrontal cortex correlated with enhanced encoding and retrieval in those listening to music. Community-dwelling humans 65 years old and older were tested initially and again in 6 months. Those who participated weekly in an hour-long music-based exercise class during the six months had decreased anxiety and gained in the executive skill of resisting interference as compared to the control group Japanese individuals 65, and older enjoyed physical exercise with musical accompaniment for one h once a week completing 40 h in 1 year. With each session, the exercise intensity gradually increased. Half of the group heard the music played in harmony with the exercise.

3.3 Music and lyrics

The other half only heard percussion that kept the beat while the people read the lyrics without music while exercising. While both groups may have appreciated gains in psychomotor speed, just the music group had significant improvement in visual spatial function. These scientists believe that cognitive functioning in elders can be enhanced when music is combined with physical exercise. To what extent is neurogenesis relevant to information processing? New brain cells in the dentate gurus are essential for discriminating little differences in experiences and sensory inputs. It is this awareness of differences in small details that pick up newness. It is during their sixth to the eighth week that new neurons are more excitable than mature brain cells permitting the plastic response of stimulated adult-born new brain cells while preserving existing neuronal function. This critical period is when intrinsic and extrinsic factors can influence the percent of new brain cells that survive and get integrated. It is also when less reliable, and exciting currents are essential to cause a plastic response such as survival, integration, memory, or long term potentiation. These new brain cells are also thought to hold associations between time-related experiences that may not lateral in content like those that occur during memory flashbacks. In their first few days of life, new brain cells grow dendrites that reach into the dentate gyrus and axons are evident. It is during this young and excitable period that new neurons require experiences such as physical activity and learning that includes challenge and newness to become integrated and stable in the dentate gyrus.

Although the many steps between birth and the connectivity that includes synaptic integration are still awaiting definition, there is almost no difference between mature brain cells and young ones by the time new neurons are about eight weeks old. While many of the steps and mechanisms of such rapid maturity are still being studied "current hypotheses suggest that it will depend on both intrinsic signaling pathways and extrinsic regulators and local network activity. "Working with adults aged 60–89 using a computer training program, the duration of and presentation speed of stimuli adapted to the skill level of the person to maintain a degree of challenge.

3.4 Improving memory

As a result of practice and challenge, individuals had improved working memory for tasks they had not trained. Pre-training and post-training electroencephalography also showed functional brain plasticity. The sample size was small (N = 32) and well educated (13–21 years of education). Further research is indicated on how to maximize the transfer of gains from training programs that are computer-based, provide adaptive challenge and can reinforce progress with greater accuracy and effectiveness than could ever be managed by human trainers. found that as little as ten 60- to 75-min sessions over a 5- to 6-week period of cognitive training helped normal elderly humans improve function on the specific skills of practice with effect sizes that were "comparable with or greater than the amount of longitudinal decline reported in previous studies;" this suggests that "these interventions have the potential to reverse age-related decline." These humans received training in reasoning, memory, or speed of processing. The computerized speed of processing training showed immediate gains regardless of age, gender, mental status, health status or education with benefits maintained over five years.

Participants have four one h booster sessions at 11 and 35 months had gains beyond those found at immediate measures and "counteracted nearly five months of normative age-related decline in processing speed." With the completion of all training and booster sessions, these people demonstrated about 2.5 standard deviations of gain in their speed of processing. Ten years after their initial training, increases were evident in the targeted cognitive skills of reasoning and speed of processing but not for memory. All participants at ten years reported less difficulty with instrumental activities of daily living. It was a randomized, controlled; single-blind trial involving 2,802 humans in six cities in the USA, the most extensive test to date. A recent small study with people 65 and older who were cognitively intact found that less daily computer associated with a lower percent of hippocampal volume. Pairing the use of these training programs with aerobic exercise could increase brain gains.

Chapter four

4.1 The Neuroplasticity with Brain

We may think that the brain, once are damaged, may not repair itself. Breakthroughs in field of neuroscience have given it, that this is not true. Though, ones neurons may be damaged beyond state of recovery, the brain stems attempts to healing itself when damaged in making new connections with new neural pathways working-around. It is called neuroplasticity the moldabilty of the brain nerves.

4.2 The grip of neuroplasticity in treatment of addiction

When one develops a habit, the brain cells create a pathway in itself which support that habit. As it engages to the habit moreover again, the pathway becomes vital and oriented. It is similar to building body through weight lifting. If you get used to lifting weights your body adapt and becomes stronger. In many modes, addiction may be explained kind of neoplastic event. The brains trained to do a particular task may it be the use alcohol hard drugs or gambling with extractives or exclusions .However, in treatment, we may retrain the brain, wicks help brain develop unique pathway that may supports recovery. With intensive therapy and other holistic interventions in brain, we try to strengthen the new the new recovery loop within the brain. The brain then adapts and enjoys recovery, those things that give people pleasure in our sober lives like family, work, interpersonal relations with people. We also retrain the brain and thus change our lives.

4.3 Brain function to the role of relapse

Importantly, in addition is the center of pleasure to the brain which is hijacked by the addictive behavior. However, it is the addictive behaviors that give out the addict a sense of joy, or may least find freedom from pain. It is not only a biochemical process which the drugs themselves affect the brain's cells biochemistry, however also a process of habit skills. The addicted brain becomes used to the addiction act for being the source of pleasure. Not only at family level, but also to job, friends, and meals the addiction affects.

We may retrain the brain and we may rebalance the addictions in various categories of biochemistry, however the old neuropath ways, and the old links of addiction and pleasure are still there. It is why we suggested having a complete abstinence alcohol and drug addicts. It does not take much time jump start the old habit. For example, you might not have gone to your college campus in ten years, but within few minutes of arrival for a visit, it starts becoming familiar to you. The old haunts and you may know how to get around. Addiction is not different to that scenario. Recovery does not remove the addiction thought process but it just gives the addict an opportunistic mode to change behaviors.

4.4 Understanding interpersonal Neuron-biology

The terminology was highlighted by Dr. Dan Siegel of UCLA. It is a Tran's disciplinary approach fathoming how the brain works. It is like weaving together understandings of why we tend behave as we do from various fields as varied as computer science, human intelligence, anthropology. Interpersonal disciplines neurobiology always helps to know two things: first, how the brain actively connect and works toward something called Neuron integration and second that the brain is defined developed to grow and heal itself in relationship to others cells.

Integration means physical wholeness. The brain wants all its disparate cells parts to work together. It is designed for you to feel enthusiastic. In recovery, we tend to help the brain reach that defined goal with whole health support.

4.5 Brain Relationship

Relationship of the brain cells also plays a significant role in mental health of an individual. Those who may be isolated may not recover as well as those who have a loving support system in place. It is not just an intuitive deduction about mental health but, there are many studies involving neuroscience, the science transplant and psychology that support this claim. Thus, to help the brain develops healthy neuropath ways and to foster recovery, we help the addict build this interpersonal support system both in treatment and beyond.

Chapter five

5.1 Sleep Medication for brain

Mice showed decreased function in the blood brain barrier with sleep deprivation). This interface between circulation and the brain is crucial to adequate supply of nutrients and oxygen to brain cells. Sleep deprivation in mice resulted in neuron inflammation in the hippocampus and associated deficits in learning and memory.

5.2 Role of sleep to metabolism energy

A primary role of sleep may be to restore brain energy metabolism since wakefulness consumes more energy particularly in gray brain matter. A study of 6,050 adults aged 65 or older found greater quality of life and independent functioning in individuals who had adequate sleep as compared to those who reported insomnia. Chronic insomnia in humans was associated with hippocampal atrophy that suggests decreased neurogenesis; this was associated with cognitive deficits .In a population of 2,822 men aged 67 and older, measured and reported sleep disturbance was associated with cognitive decline. A review found that accumulated sleep deprivation and sleep fragmentation greater than 24 h was associated with a decrease in neurogenesis that was not quickly reversible.

5.3 Diffusion reduction

Seventeen people that had never complied with treatment of chronic obstructive sleep apnea showed "diffuse reduction" in white brain matter integrity that was associated with cognitive dysfunction as measured with neuropsychological testing .However, after 1 year of compliance with treatment, brain pathology has improved significantly along with "significant improvements involving memory, attention, and executive-functioning." Memory deficits and mood effects noted with sleep deprived humans may have some association with impaired neurogenesis. Chronic sleep deprivation in animals resulted in increased inflammatory molecules and decreased BDNF which is crucial to many components of neuroplasticity. A recent review of animal research concludes that the major physiological challenge created by sleep deprivation can include cognitive deficits, inflammation, and general impairment of protein translation, metabolic imbalance, and thermal deregulation. Sleep is essential for removal of waste and distribution of glucose, lipids, amino acids, growth factors, and neuromodulators. One of the neuroprotective mechanisms of adequate sleep may be its reduction of inflammation that can be associated with aging as well as with decreased neurogenesis as observed in animal models. However, when one night of sleep deprivation in rats included gentle handling to prevent sleep, neurogenesis increased significantly initially as well as 15 and 30 days later We are gifted to be alive in the age of technology; to have decades of research on neuroplasticity; to have an increasing database on evidence-based interventions associated with improving health; and to read findings suggesting that age-related cognitive decline may be slowed, arrested or even reversed.

Some of the most convincing and compelling research comes from animal studies showing the capacity of positive interventions to drive neuroplasticity in a positive direction. had already found significant gains in brain architecture and performance in rats when she responded to the challenge that they were not elderly by adding an impactful intervention; technicians removed rats from their cage, held them and talked to them. The result of this "TLC" was 50% increase in lifespan to the equivalent of 90 human years. Perhaps most important, rats continued to show brain gains across this longer lifespan; Diamond opined that humans could appreciate these same brain gains at any age. Equally convincing on the value of the power of positives is the work by Rather than finding the usual detrimental effects of sleep deprivation, gentle handling of rats to prevent sleep was associated with significant increases in neurogenesis initially, 15 days later and 30 days later. Caution is essential in generalizing these findings to humans. Based on animal research it was assumed that neurogenesis declines rapidly after a certain age.

5.4 Neurogenesis

Humans show fewer declines in neurogenesis with aging and still produce 700 new brain cells in each hippocampus each day, according to innovative research using Carbon-14 dating. The rate of neurogenesis in animals and in humans has been increased by factors including aerobic exercise and sustained fivefold with long-term environmental enrichment. Human research might consider the impact of some form of "TLC" such as using one hand to massage the other hand during those over-night flights, night shift work or other circumstances that include sleep deprivation. An example of neoplastic flexibility in humans is the "significant improvements involving memory, attention, and executive-functioning" after 1 year of compliance with CPAP treatment in people whose previous non-compliance with treatment of sleep apnea showed "diffuse reduction" in white brain matter integrity that was associated with cognitive dysfunction .Even though this was a small sample, it might help clinicians influence motivation and empower clients to increase healthy sleep for brain health.

5.5 Molecule circulation

Essential molecules for health must circulate in adequate supply to the brain and waste products that could have toxic impact must be removed for best brain performance and maintenance. That is part of the critical function of sleep as shown in research on the lymphatic system. Building on animal research on neuroplasticity gains associated with exercise, the finding of "effectively reversing age-related loss in volume by 1–2 years" in the hippocampus and prefrontal cortex with associated improvements in memory might also increase motivation. Coupled with multiple other studies showing improvements in brain chemistry, architecture, and performance this body of research is an invitation to apply concepts and techniques in clinical practice to educate as well as increase treatment compliance with this and other non-pharmacological interventions that can be powerful, portable, and inexpensive ways of enhancing brain chemistry and architecture while improving general health. Human research has the added advantage of considering the impact of thought alone. Whether long term meditation for tens of thousands of hours or short term for 4 weeks, structural and functional neuroplasticity have been observed. Although calorie restriction and some nutrients have been associated with increased healthy longevity in many species, this could require greater creativity in motivating individuals to eat less and eat differently. Educating people that some cognitive and general health benefits could be related to the resultant reduction in inflammation and oxidative damage may not be enough.

More research on the Okinawa Program should be encouraged because the World Health Organization declared Okinawa a centenarian center of the world based on the percentage of Okinawans that remained physically, socially and cognitively intact well past the age of 100, a distinction that persisted until Western lifestyle choices markedly changed that demographic. With the growing global burden of obesity and associated negative health impacts, clinicians could play pivotal roles in empowering people to celebrate benefits of *haram* for their brain health; to structure reinforcement schedules for adherence to healthier food choices; and to learn from the Okinawan model that led to remarkable vigorous longevity.

Chapter six

6.1 Physical Exercises enhancing brain performance

It is clear that physical exercise prescriptions need to be part of healthcare to enhance brain health. Without such, the harms that can accrue are similar to those of smoking and obesity. Found that, independent of vascular risk factors, low or no leisure physical activity associated with more significant decline in processing speed and episodic memory across five years as compared to individuals with moderate to the heavy intensity of physical exercise. Regular exercise can reinvigorate the immune system. In elders without known cognitive impairment exercise can improve cognitive performance.

Being aerobic up to 60 min can improve information processing. A recent review suggests that different types of physical activity and a high level of physical fitness can decrease the so-called "normal age-related" atrophy of the hippocampus and increase the volume of the hippocampus. With elders whose average age was 83, it predicted greater integrity in microstructures in brain networks related to memory. It can result in higher health of brain white matter in people aged 60–78.Exercise energizes motor responses to improve the speed of reaction — aerobic exercise associated with increased neurogenesis in humans.

6.2 Exercise influence

Exercise influences the survival and maturation of adult-born neurons. In community dwellers between the ages of 55 and 80, physical activity was a powerful method to increase gray matter volume in the hippocampus and prefrontal cortex "effectively reversing age-related loss in volume by 1–2 years" with related improvements in memory performance. Six months of high-intensity aerobic exercise with women between the ages of 55 and 85 who had mild cognitive decline was a potent non-pharmacologic treatment that improved their performance on multiple tests of executive functioning.

A review of randomized controlled trials suggested that physical exercise could be a powerful way to increase gray brain matter in elders such that cognitive losses and behavioral problems associated with brain atrophy prevention. It may have pervasive benefits that could translate into less risk in humans for Alzheimer's disease. All things put into consideration, and it is URGENT to prescribe exercise at any age because it regarded as beneficial for the body and brain. There is no reason to hold back on these prescriptions while evolving research attempts to establish guidelines on preferred dose, timing, and method. In the Cardiovascular Health Study, calorie expenditure measured along with assessments of cognitive functioning and MRI measurements of brain volume in individuals with an average age of 78.3. Their findings suggest "that simply caloric expenditure, regardless of type or duration of exercise, may alone moderate neurodegeneration and even increase GM volume in structures of the brain central to cognitive functioning."

6.3 Diet and Inflammation

Total intake of food and fluid, the frequency of consumption and content consumed all factor into the molecular events of energy metabolism and neuroplasticity. The optimal combination of nutrients can be a practical way of enhancing cognitive performance while increasing the health span. Given the scope of this review, full coverage of all pertinent research is not possible in this writing. This writing intends to highlight several dietary choices that could be neuroprotective could have positive effects on neuroplasticity including on adult neurogenesis and could influence the reduction of chronic inflammation which has a deleterious impact on brain health and function.

Calorie restriction with adequate nutrients has been associated with health benefits through increased longevity in organisms from yeast to flies, worms, and mammals. Research suggests that Hara hachi bu, or "eat until you are 80% full," has been an essential factor in exceptional longevity with increased health span for one human population.

6.4 Cognitive power and general health

Reducing calories, 30% was associated with an average of 20% improvement in verbal memory after three months. Some of these cognitive and general health benefits of calorie restriction in humans are thought to be related to the reduction of inflammation and oxidative damage. The brain and body interaction in response to the limitation of calories could influence the sleep cycle which has linked with inflammation; and it might be related to "the global metabolic reprogramming of the central biological clock" Still, the little nuances of the calorie restriction remains poorly understood. The problem with low-grade inflammation that can be chronic as well as undiagnosed is that association with decreased cognitive functioning with aging. Intermittent fasting in animals found benefits that equaled or exceeded the benefits of calorie restriction; brain cells in these animals were more capable of resisting the injury of an injection into the hippocampus that has known toxic effects. Reducing caloric intake seems to improve synaptic resilience to damage and modify the number, architecture, and performance of synapses. A reduction in inflammation with better preservation of cognitive function in animals with sepsis suggested that intermittent fasting can induce adaptive responses systemically as well as in the brain.

Each requires healthy nutrition. Whether that uses the Okinawan Diet, that was one of the factors in the lives of high-functioning centenarians or the Mediterranean Diet, which has some evidence for being "a potential strategy to reduce cognitive decline in older age," is discretionary. Since both emphasize vegetables, fruits, fish as a source of protein, and low glycemic load, both would be rich in polyphenols and the healthier polyunsaturated fats and would have antioxidant and anti-inflammatory benefits. Interestingly, the polyphenol resveratrol also increases longevity while preserving memory and hippocampal microstructure. This polyphenol occurs naturally in grapes, purple grape juice and some berries such as blueberries and cranberries. Other invaluable polyphenols that get much more full dietary acceptance are the flavonoids found in cocoa which are noted for powerful anti-inflammatory as well as antioxidant effects.

6.5 Flexibility of blood vessels

The added benefits of these flavonoids are the dose-dependent improved blood flow to the brain as well as increased health and flexibility of blood vessels A recent review of the neuroprotective effects of the flavonoids in cocoa suggested that they "provoke angiogenesis, neurogenesis, and changes in neuron morphology, mainly in regions involved in learning and memory." Another review similarly found that cocoa flavonoids are neuroprotective and can enhance mood and cognitive function. Humans aged 50–69 years who consumed 900 mg of cocoa flavones daily for three months enjoyed improved dentate gyros performance on cognitive testing as well as on fMRI Curcuma is a neuroprotective polyphenol with anti-inflammatory and antioxidant capacity that can increase differentiation of neural stem cells into neurons in rats. It has shown an ability to enhance neurogenesis and increase the number of neural stem cells in the hippocampus of adult mice.

Healthy humans aged 60–85 appreciated improvements in cognition and mood. Also crucial to optimal central nervous system structure and function are the essential omega-3 fatty acids eicosapentaenoic acid (EPA) and docosahexaenoic acid (DHA; which humans cannot create. Primary sources include fish and plant foods. Interestingly, in the parts of the brain essential to cognition and memory one study found increased gray matter volumes that associated with fish consumption and independent of plasma measures of omega-3 fatty acids, highlighting the complexity of, and interactions of, dietary impact in humans.

An animal study found that a diet early in life that was high in omega-3 fatty acids protected brain cells from environmental challenges later in life. When these animals transitioned from high omega-3s to a Western diet, the "epigenetic memory" protected these animals from cognitive decline. In the Framingham Heart Study, people whose DHA level was in the top quartile had a highly significant 47% lower risk for developing dementia. A random controlled trial that supplemented with fish oil found "increased red blood cell omega-3 content, working memory performance, and BOLD signal in the posterior cingulate cortex during greater working memory load in older adults with subjective memory impairment." Thus they suggested that supplementing with omega-3 fish oil could enhance brain cell response to challenges in working memory. A research review indicates that a high brain concentration of DHA can optimize synaptic plasticity and efficiency and help maintain homeostasis in the synapses. For efficient transmission of data between brain cells, the plasma membrane must remain fluid. DHA is a component of this membrane.

Rats maintained on a mixture of alpha-linolenic, and linoleic acid showed enhanced learning that the researchers opined was due to the fatty acids changing the amount of cholesterol in the membrane of the neurons. Adequate intake of the essential fatty acids is crucial to maintaining the fluid transmission of molecules across neuronal membranes because this is where much of the action takes place for such core brain functions as learning, memory, and sleep.They are also essential in building the myelin sheath that enhances the efficient processing of information. The finding that DHA is vulnerable to oxidative damage underscores both the need for polyphenols as well as the complexity of the interactive neuroplastic influence of the several components of the dietary intervention matrix which also needs to consider essential vitamins and minerals. For example, since brain health requires adequate Vitamin B12, indirect measures of this status are recommended.

Chapter seven

7.1 Aging in harmony

7.1.1 why the third act of life should be musical

It's never too late to pick up a musical instrument. There are many reasons why it's a great idea, particularly in old age.

We usually hear about reasons to increase music education for children and a good cause. There are social benefits and cognitive to playing an instrument that aid a child's development. Consequently, as an older adult, there are long-term effects of having taken part in these musical activities, as it can decline to cognitive limits.

7.1.2 Music for health and wellbeing

Often, the worry is that playing an instrument will be too difficult for older adults to manage. On the contrary, learning to play an instrument can provide a great sense of goals and satisfaction.

Older adults relish the opportunity of learning new.

Cognitive benefits aside, music can also be great social activities for adults, facilitating social bonding and decreasing feelings of loneliness or isolation.

Music programs linked to improvements measured in Immune body systems such as the presence of antibodies and vital signs of heart rate/blood pressure.

It's a suggestion that this is a consequence of decreases in stress that can happen when taking part in musical activities.

However, further research is needed to determine exactly how this relationship functions.

Even training can have long-lasting effects. But this doesn't mean that those who have never played an instrument in childhood have missed the boat. The developing brain is plastic: that says it can learn new things all the time. So, should we consider an increase in music programs for those in the third age?

7.2 Music as a workout for the fingers

Learning to play an instrument such as the piano involves many complex finger sequencing and coordination tasks. As such, it can be an excellent test-bed for learning to move fingers independently.

The creativity of music and the enjoyment people take in playing is particularly crucial for rehabilitation, as it encourages continued practice leading ultimately to higher benefits.

It's thanks to this that piano lessons have been used to successfully retrain hand function for stroke patient The immediate auditory feedback from each finger movement is thought to help adults movement error reduction and work towards moving at a more regular pace.

Music training is an excellent environment to train cognitive and motor abilities, both in the contexts of child development and for rehabilitation. The question for older adults is this: can learn a musical instrument not only put the brakes on cognitive and motor decline but allow development of new skills?

Older adults can motor learning that is, they can improve their rate of learning new things – and the best environments for brain training are ones that are a flexible trend.

Of course, many activities can be novels such as juggling or knitting, but the advantages of learning an instrument may be found in the breadth of skills required to play. At Western Sydney University, we are currently investigating how piano training can be used with healthy older adults to improve their general hand function in unrelated daily tasks.

7.3 Playing music as a workout for the brain

Learning to play a musical instrument is an extremely complex task that involves the coordination of multiple sensory systems within the brain. Many devices require precise coordination between the eyes, the ears, and the hands to play a musical note. Use the resulting sound, as feedback, the brain prepares for the next, and so it continues. The act of music-making is quite a brain workout.

The relationship between the motor and auditory parts of the brain is strengthened when physically playing music. It may explain why adults trained to perform certain melodies have a musical enhancement in mind compared to adults only trained to listen to the same songs.

As playing music involves many different parts of the brain, even a short-term program for older adult musical novices can lead to generalized improvements for ability cognition.

Music for all

It's vital to understand how we can aid the current generation of older adults, in terms of both health and personal enjoyment. With the myriad benefits provided by playing a musical instrument, it would seem beneficial to have a wider variety of musical activities on offer to the older generation.

Wouldn't it be great if the third age wasn't viewed as a final descent from some mid-life peak, but some new act of life that opens up these opportunities? Perhaps we should give older adults the chance to develop in ways they could never have imagined before.

Activities such as singing in a choir, or playing the piano can provide this opportunity, as well as offering many general benefits to health and wellbeing.

So whether it's in independent living, retirement or assisted care, let's make the third act of life a musical one!

Chapter eight

8.0 What does neuroscience have to do with coaching and therapy?

The neuroscience is related to the central nervous system which stimulates body reaction since there the body information transferred

If you are a coach or therapist, your job is to facilitate change in your client's

- ➤ **Thinking:** beliefs and attitudes always regulates the mind functionality
- ➤ **Emotions:** Being more mindfulness and resilience to what you are doing bring effective change
- ➤ **Behavior new healthy habits** give out new adaptation and with time a significant improvement
- ➤ **Coaching therapy** builds the mental skills needed to support lasting change. Skills such as resilience
- ➤ **Mindfulness;** which sustain upward mobility of the success
- ➤ **Self-awareness;** It helps great realization to what extent your potential can reach
- ➤ **Motivation:** keep engrossed in achieving the target set
- ➤ **Resilience;** Being aware of the changes that happen in your new environment
- ➤ **Optimism** It helps to have speculative hopes of a good trend
- ➤ **Critical thinking;** Helps in making an essential decision at various stage

> **Stress management;** helps to deal with
> life challenges

Health and wellness coaching mostly are emerging as powerful interventions to help people initiate and maintain sustainable change.

How May neuroscience more deeply informs coaching and therapy?

Back in the mid-1980s when I was in grad school, I started looking at neuroscience as a basis of NLP & Hypnosis and the why and how it worked. Thomas Jessell. Kandel won the 2000 Nobel prize in Physiology or Medicine for his research on memory storage in neurons.prize in Physiology or Medicine for his research on memory storage in neurons.

A few years before getting his Nobel, Kindle wrote a paper new intellectual framework. The paper explained how neuroscience could provide a new view of mental health and wellbeing and fitness.

Based on Knelling paper, researchers at the Yale School of Medicine proposed seven principles of brain-based therapy for psychiatrists, psychologists and therapists. The policies have been given a new translation into practical applications for health & wellness, business, and life coaches.

8.2 fundamental principle

1. All mental processes, mostly complex psychological processes, derive from the operation of the brain.
2. In so far as psychotherapy or counseling is effective. It presumably does so through cognitive learning, by producing changes in gene expression that alters the strength of synapse contentions.

That is, human neural interactions and experience influence how the brain works.

The concept of brain change is now well established in neuroscience and often referred to as neuroplasticity. Ample neuroscience authentic research supports the idea that our brains remain adaptable throughout our lifespan mode. Here is a summative look of Kindle, Cappers and colleagues thoughts on how neuroscience applied to therapy and coaching.

Some principles of neuroscience every coach should know

8.3 Memories are not perfect

Our memories never a perfect account of what happened. Memories are re-written each time when we recalled them depending on how, when and where we were retrieving nodes.

For example, a query, photograph and a particular scent can interact with a memory resulting in it modified as it reclaimed.

With a significant trend in life experience we narratives into their memories Autobiography memories that tell, the stories of our lives are always undergoing revision smooth because our sense of self is too.

Consciously or not, we use indications to reinvent our past, and with it, our present and future.

8.4 Emotion underlies memory formation

Memories and emotions are interconnected neural nerves processes.

The amygdala which plays major a role in emotional arousal mediates neurotransmitters essential for memory consolidation. Emotional arousal can activate the amygdala, which in turn modulates the storage of memory.

8.5 Relationships are the foundation for vital growth

Relationships in childhood and adulthood have the enacted power to elicit positive change.

Sometimes it takes the love, care or attention of just one person to help another change for the better.

The therapeutic relationship can help clients modify neural systems and enhance emotional regulation.

8.6 Nature and natural win

Genetically making and the environment interactivity in the brain shapes our minds and influential look.

Therapy or coaching may be thought of as a strategic and purposeful environmental tool to facilitate change and maybe efficiency and of shaping neural pathways.

8.7 Experiences transforming the CNS

The areas of our brain associated with emotions, memories such as the pre-frontal cortex of the brain, the amygdala, and the hippocampus are not hard-wired they are plastic

Research suggests each of us constructs feelings from a diversity of sources, our physiological state, by our reactions to the outside environment, experiences and learning, and our culture and upbringing.

8.8 Imagining and doing are the same as the brain functionality

Mental imagery and visualization not only act the same brain regions as the actual behavior but also may speed up the learning of a new skill.

Envisioning a very different life mode may as successfully invoke change as the experience.

8.9 We don't always know how or what our brain is thinking

Unconscious processes exert a significant influence on our thoughts actions feelings.

The brain may process nonverbal and unconscious information, and information handled unconsciously can still influence therapeutic and other relationships. Reacting to unconscious perceptions without consciously understanding the reaction is possible.

Chapter Nine

9.1 The Neurology Why Non-conformists Look Alike?

You ever notice that subgroups all have a very similar look, and have for as long as we can remember? The hippies with flower shirts and jeans,the disco crowd with super tight pants and styled hair? The biker look,The current "hipster" with beard and shaved side hair and long on top?

9.1.1 The answer lies in your neurology and neuro-plasticity.

Anti-conformists have an odd way of ending up looking like each other.

A Brandeis mathematician looks at how this synchronicity occurs.

Understanding the mechanism behind non-conformist conformity has applications in other areas, like the stock market.We're here for such a short time, and we'd like to think we matter. It is the drive to be significant, to stand out, this is deep in your neurology passed down through thousands of generations. "I'm not just one more person — I'm different." That's true, and also... not. We're very much like one another, though the particular details of our lives are, of course, pretty unique. Still, particularly in the Western world, we like to be seen as separate from — and better than? — the herd. Many of us go out of our way to look different than "them," too, declaring our uniqueness in our appearance.

The interesting thing is also going on at the deep neurological level (not just subconscious but actually in your DNA, is the need to survive and thought history if one was too far out of mainstream, you died and your gene pool stopped. The "lone wolf" gets killed.

So, this is how come so many individual anti-conformists end up looking alike It's called the "hipster effect," and a study from Brandeis University mathematician _explains how it happens.

It's not just an issue of visual fashion, by the way. As Touboul tell technology review, "Beyond the choice of the best suit to wear this winter, this study may have important implications in understanding synchronization of nerve cells, investment strategies in finance, or emergent dynamics in social science."

9.2 DNA

This is what we in NLP and Hypnosis would call mirror and matching, we want to break away, but get in some group, at least somewhat in order to survive.

There is some thought that also in some select individuals DNA is the drive to break away, this is how new groups are made, and new subgroups, but the leaders of the break away are soon surrounded by people attempting to duplicate the "individualist" but need a model to follow. Thus the growth of all the subgroups, hipsters, bikers, hippies, greasers, jocks, goth, cowboy, the corporate look, and the like.

One only needs to look to NLP to see this in action the group, NLP, was founded by rebels, and were hippies at heart, and most of the core group modeled that. When you went to an early training (I can attest to this) people looked this way, and if you did not you were somewhat pushed away. Then when Tony Robbins broke on the scene he created a break away from the break away, blue suit white shirt, red tie, suspenders and many followed that. We still see it in Hypnosis and NLP....

9.3 Personal brand

While anti-conformists may, at first, succeed in devising their own personal brand of sartorial rebelliousness, it's followed by an inevitable, if unintentional, synchronization around a single type appearance. Touboul's study looks at how such people seem to inevitably become synchronized. They mirror and match at the subconscious level. He suspects that a major influence on the way it happens may be the speed of propagation of styles through a culture.

We want to be different, but there are no neuro cells, or neuro pathways for you to follow, but when you see one, it is easier to follow and model that.

Not everyone learns about or adopts new styles in the same way. Some follow fashion closely, some go by word of mouth, and some emulate the appearance of well-known individuals they admire. In the latter case, the tipping-point may occur after a mutually-revered celebrity adopts a new fashion. Many can remember when Michael Jordan shaved his head, which was rare at time, now it is common.

This is why you see the look from small towns, to the inner city. It becomes a focal point of your identity

Right now we see it in the "stubble" five o'clock shadow look that men have, at first it was bold, different now we see it everywhere. I am amused when I see it in film where active military and FBI agents will have that "look" when in reality that is not seen.

In Touboul's simple model, one is either a member of the mainstream or a hipster, and he explores different hipster-to-mainstream ratios. He also factors in different amounts of time it might take a hipster to detect a new style and respond to it.

Simple as his model is, Touboul has found that experimenting with those two factors produces a surprisingly complex set of behaviors, though synchronization always occurs. Even when he revises his model to allow for more than two types of people, synchronization still occurs.

One could also look at the explosion of tattoo's, at one time was a rarely seen thing. Military, bikers, prisoners, then we started seeing it everywhere. To the point when if one does not have "tats" people are surprised. We shall see what happens with this when the trend dies out for unlike redoing your hair, fashion, or shaving, the effect is harder to change.

Often, of course, roles may swap when there are so many hipsters that they become the mainstream. "For example," says Touboul, "if a majority of individuals shave their beard, then most hipsters will want to grow a beard, and if this trend propagates to a majority of the population, it will lead to new, synchronized, switch to shaving." An odd sudden swap occurs when the number of mainstreamers and hipsters is roughly equal — everybody winds up switching together between different trends.

The rebels must rebel.....

We see this now in NLP where Richard Bandler, one of the genius's behind NLP, he who usually wore a tee shirt and jeans now wears a suit often when training, and Tony Robbins who went the other way from suits, to shorts, and jeans when he is at his training.

So what is your rebel look or do you follow a path, when I went back to my western (redneck) roots people asked why I changed, maybe I was rebelling or I just like the look.

Chapter Ten

ADDENDUMS

10.1 Improving the Potential of Neuroplasticity

A fundamental principle of neuronal plasticity is that synchronous or asynchronous activity in neurons can lead, respectively, to strengthening or weakening of shared synapses. Breech asked whether paired associative stimulation (PAS) of interconnected areas of the cortex via noninvasive Tran's cranial magnetic stimulation (TMS) might selectively induce Habana-like plasticity in a specific anatomical pathway in humans.

10.2 Neuroplasticity induction

As introduced by Stefan PAS is a plasticity-inducing protocol that pairs electrical stimulation of a median nerve with a TMS pulse over primary motor cortex (M1). The time interval between stimuli is crucial for induction of either potentiation- or depression-like plasticity effects. The polarity of the effect is dependent on whether the input to the cortex from the median nerve stimulation precedes, coincides with, or follows the TMS-induced motor output. The motor output is measured as the motor-evoked potential (MEP).

Subsequently, Rizzo developed the idea of PAS between cortical regions. They demonstrated that it is possible to induce lasting changes in paired-pulse inter hemispheric motor inhibition and single-pulse-induced M1-MEP size in humans by using a modified PAS protocol that used two consecutive TMS pulses between left and right M1.

To address whether such plasticity between interconnected cortical areas can be pathway-specific, used an established paired-pulse protocol (with an interstimulus interval of 8 ms) for probing physiological connectivity between ventral premotor cortex (PMv) and M1. A first conditioning TMS pulse is applied over PMv followed by a second test TMS pulse over M1. The effect is measured and quantified as the change between the MEP produced by the test pulse alone and the MEP produced when the test pulse is influenced by the conditioning pulse. They then sought to induce plastic change in this connection by repetitively delivering 90 pairs of pulses (one pair every 10 s) with the same interstimulus interval (ISI) and the same coil positions.

Bunch found that stimulating PMv and M1 with an ISI of 8 ms significantly potentiated the inhibitory effect in the PMv–M1 paired-pulse paradigm, as the test-MEP size was reduced significantly. The effects of the PAS on functional connectivity were present for up to 1 h after intervention and reverted back to baseline at 3 h.To demonstrate the pathway specificity of this plasticity, the authors used a second stimulation site, the pre-supplementary area (pre-SMA), which was targeted by moving 4 cm anterior to the vertex. In conditions, PMv and pre-SMA PAS, 110% M1 resting motor threshold (rMT) was used as the stimulation intensity. The results support an anatomical pathway specificity of the plasticity-inducing protocol: paired stimulation over the pre-SMA was not effective, i.e., it did not change PMv–M1 connectivity, whereas PMv stimulation induced lasting effects.

10.3 Cognitive state

As a control experiment for the timing component of the plasticity-inducing protocol, the order of stimulation was switched between connected areas. The effect was seen only with the correct order of stimulation, i.e., with premotor stimulation preceding M1 stimulation.

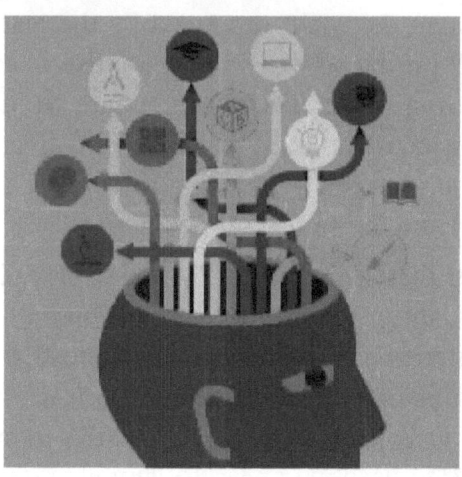

Interestingly, also tested whether the plasticity induced, in the pathways depended on the cognitive state of the subject at the time of testing. Previous studies indicated that the effect of this connectivity depends on the cognitive state of the subject. While the PMv–M1 connection is inhibitory when the subject is at rest, endogenous activation of the pathway during grasping causes the connection to become excitatory. The polarity of the induced plasticity indeed depended on the cognitive state of the subject: inhibitory effects were induced when subjects were at rest, whereas excitatory effects were induced when the subject was engaged in a vasomotor task.

The strength of the paper lies in establishing that a specific pathway from PMv to M1 is strengthened in a targeted manner by TMS, selectively functionally activated by the grasp task, and is altered in a process analogous to PAS. Nonetheless, some anatomical and temporal aspects of the method need to be addressed to strengthen these claims.

To conclude anatomical specificity of the PMv stimulation on the basis of a lack of response from SMA assumes that both areas are being adequately stimulated. There are technical problems with ensuring adequate comparable levels of stimulation when delivering TMS at 110% of M1 resting motor threshold to PMv and pre-SMA. One method that seeks to ensure adequate stimulation of SMA uses an alternative coil orientation, determines anatomical location relative to motor cortex leg area, and uses a high stimulation intensity comparable to leg threshold to ensure stimulation penetrates to a suitable depth. Stimulating pre-SMA at a scalp location 4 cm anterior to vertex, and using 110% M1 rMT, may not provide a comparable level of stimulation to that obtained by stimulating a more accessible structure defined according to individual anatomy. Furthermore, Grappa found that the optimal intensity to use for the premotor conditioning stimulus in paired-pulse experiments varies between subjects. It would be useful to test the effect of varying stimulation intensity on the effect of the plasticity protocol used.

There are practical difficulties with delivering dual-site TMS to PMv and M1. Using coils in close apposition, as did, necessitates some compromise in optimal coil position and orientation, because space on the scalp is limited. This compromise affects the anatomical precision of stimulation. One solution to the problem of using dual-site premotor-to-M1 stimulation is the use of specialized mini-coils with decentralized coil windings to maximize anatomical specificity. Eccentric sites of maximal stimulation distant from the coil center and asymmetrically complementary between test and conditioning coil allow 3–4 cm distance between stimulation sites with optimal coil orientation maintained. Even though observed no direct effect of PMv stimulation alone, the coil position and orientation used for PMv may make direct current spread to M1 more likely in the PMv–M1 condition. This may not be of great importance in considering responses in paired-pulse experiments, but when plasticity is induced through repetitive stimulation, thought must be given to whether the stimulation of PMv really achieves its M1 effect through the precise circuit proposed. Early paired-pulse studies suggested transition from inhibition to excitation of M1 MEPs with increasing intensity of premotor conditioning stimulus. Applied a conditioning stimulus to PMv and reported excitation of the M1 test response at 80% active-motor threshold, but inhibition at 90% resting-motor threshold. If current spread from premotor stimulation progressively alters M1 threshold, this may alter interpretation of the polarity changes attributed to the functional task in the described plasticity protocol.

10.4 Stimulation

There are also timing issues, relating both to the task used by and to the concept of paired-associative plasticity, that require some thought. The task required many cognitive processes involving motor cortex to be active at the time of stimulation. Timing of the delivery of TMS amid the cognitive processes involved with pressing a touch bar; surveying a visual scene; attending and responding to auditory and visual stimuli; preparing and releasing reach, grasp, and lift; all make it difficult to be sure the functional aspects of the experiment are purely relating to grasp, or that stimulation occurs at the optimal time. Another aspect of timing is establishing that the interstimulus interval is correct for the circuit proposed. Other studies have shown that the effect on the MEP greatly depends on the ISI in this context. tested different interstimulus intervals between PMv conditioning and M1 test pulse and found the effect to vary, being maximal at 4 and 6 ms. Knowing the dependence of the effect on the ISI, it would be useful to test different appropriate intervals. It does not follow that the optimal interstimulus interval for a PMv–M1 effect should also be optimal for pre-SMA–M1. Furthermore, in established PAS protocols, the interstimulus interval is critical for the polarity of the plasticity effect. If a corticocortical PAS is proposed, then a critical part of testing the theory should be testing the effect with different interstimulus intervals. These issues could be addressed by extending the currently used protocol and, for example, combining TMS-induced changes with multimodal approaches such as functional imaging (dynamic causal modeling) to verify changes in connectivity strength between specific cortical areas.

10.5 Nervous system in neuroplasticity

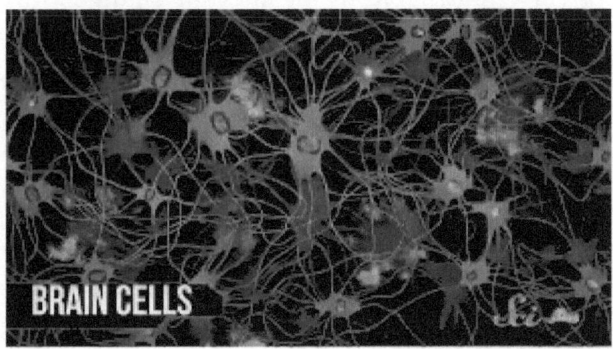

Neuroplasticity is defined as the ability of the nervous system to respond to extrinsic or intrinsic stimuli by a reorganization of its function, structure, or connections. It has a significant functional, but also a therapeutic, role across brain diseases, as well as in health. It can be experience-driven, is time-sensitive, and it is influenced by the environment and internal states, such as motivation and attention. Not all plasticity has a positive impact on clinical or behavioral status. It might in fact have negative consequences, a phenomenon called "maladaptive plasticity," which has been demonstrated in animal and human research. There is a need for sophisticated methods to promote plasticity within specific networks or pathways. For example, consider therapeutic intervention after brain injury and the treatment of neglect syndromes. This requires pathways to be targeted with great specificity since multiple functional pathways controlling the motor areas deriving from parietal cortex are disrupted. Other complex disorders, such as neuropsychiatric states, are not characterized by a localized lesion, but by abnormalities in distributed neural circuits such as limbic, front striatal, etc. The idea that these targets, which are currently impossible to target with noninvasive plasticity inducing paradigms, might be selectively modifiable by promoting changes through a combination with specific cognitive states is attractive. Following the approach presented and others, it is appealing to speculate that endogenous brain activity might, in theory, even serve as one of the stimuli of Hebbian plasticity.

The current paper is an important example of trying to improve and tailor plasticity-inducing strategies, while it also demonstrates that there is still plenty of work in the field to be done.